MONSTER Trucks

by Nick Gordon

BELLWETHER MEDIA • MINNEAPOLIS, MN

Note to Librarians, Teachers, and Parents:

Blastoff! Readers are carefully developed by literacy experts and combine standards-based content with developmentally appropriate text.

Level 1 provides the most support through repetition of high-frequency words, light text, predictable sentence patterns, and strong visual support.

Level 2 offers early readers a bit more challenge through varied simple sentences, increased text load, and less repetition of high-frequency words.

Level 3 advances early-fluent readers toward fluency through increased text and concept load, less reliance on visuals, longer sentences, and more literary language.

Level 4 builds reading stamina by providing more text per page, increased use of punctuation, greater variation in sentence patterns, and increasingly challenging vocabulary.

Level 5 encourages children to move from "learning to read" to "reading to learn" by providing even more text, varied writing styles, and less familiar topics.

Whichever book is right for your reader, Blastoff! Readers are the perfect books to build confidence and encourage a love of reading that will last a lifetime!

This edition first published in 2014 by Bellwether Media, Inc.

No part of this publication may be reproduced in whole or in part without written permission of the publisher. For information regarding permission, write to Bellwether Media, Inc., Attention: Permissions Department, 5357 Penn Avenue South, Minneapolis, MN 55419.

Library of Congress Cataloging-in-Publication Data

Gordon, Nick.
 Monster trucks / by Nick Gordon.
  pages cm. – (Blastoff! readers: Monster machines)
 Summary: "Developed by literacy experts for students in kindergarten through grade three, this book introduces monster trucks to young readers through leveled text and related photos"–Provided by publisher.
 Audience: K-3
 Includes bibliographical references and index.
 ISBN 978-1-60014-940-5 (hardcover : alkaline paper)
 1. Monster trucks–Juvenile literature. 2. Racing trucks–Juvenile literature. 3. Stunt driving–Juvenile literature. I. Title.
 TL230.15.G6736 2014
 629.224–dc23
                                                              2013007616

Printed in the United States of America, North Mankato, MN.

Table of
Contents

Monster Trucks!

Monster trucks race along tracks. Their tires kick up mud.

Monster trucks
also speed over
big jumps.

Monster Parts

Monster trucks have big parts. Their tires are taller than a kid!

Sometimes monster trucks flip. Strong **roll cages** protect drivers.

roll cage

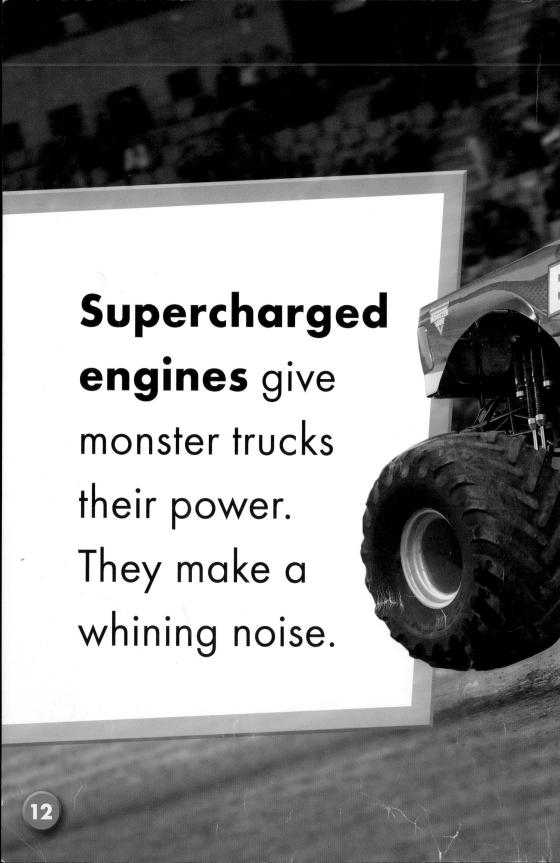

Supercharged engines give monster trucks their power. They make a whining noise.

supercharged
engine

Wild Tricks

Monster trucks
do wild tricks.
They turn in circles
to do **donuts**.

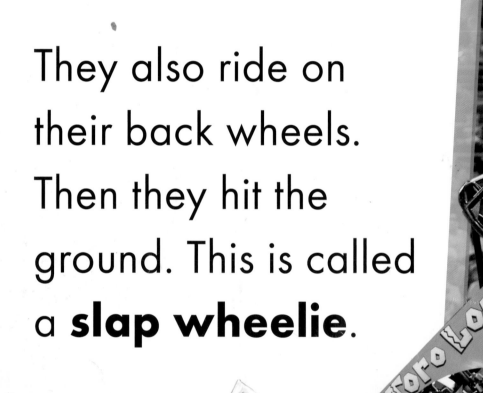

They also ride on their back wheels. Then they hit the ground. This is called a **slap wheelie**.

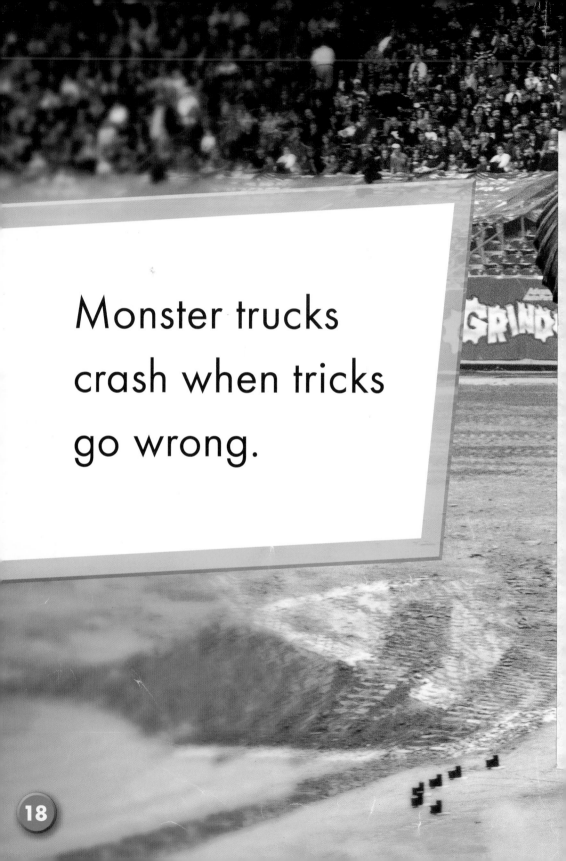

Monster trucks crash when tricks go wrong.

Fans cheer
when drivers
get out safely.
What a thrill!

Glossary

donuts—tricks in which a truck spins in place

roll cages—strong metal bars that protect drivers during crashes

slap wheelie—a trick in which a truck's front tires are in the air and then slam to the ground

supercharged engines—the parts of some vehicles that produce power with the help of superchargers; superchargers allow fuel to burn more quickly.

To Learn More

AT THE LIBRARY

Nelson, Kristin L. *Monster Trucks*. Minneapolis, Minn.: Lerner Publications, 2011.

Peppas, Lynn. *Monster Trucks*. New York, N.Y.: Crabtree Pub. Co., 2012.

Wiseman, Blaine. *Monster Trucks*. New York, N.Y.: Weigl Publishers, 2011.

ON THE WEB

Learning more about monster trucks is as easy as 1, 2, 3.

1. Go to www.factsurfer.com.

2. Enter "monster trucks" into the search box.

3. Click the "Surf" button and you will see a list of related Web sites.

With factsurfer.com, finding more information is just a click away.

Index

The images in this book are reproduced through the courtesy of: Maksim Shmeljov, front cover; Natursports, pp. 4-5, 6-7, 12-13; Sergei Bachlakov Xinhua News Agency/ Newscom, pp. 8-9; SMI/ Newscom, pp. 10-11, 14-15; Associated Press, p. 13 (small); Daniel Goncalves/ Cal Sport Media/ Newscom, pp. 16-17; Juan DeLeon/ SCG/ Zumapress.com/ Newscom, pp. 18-19, 20-21.